It always seems impossible until it's done

7 Secrets of building a million dollar empire

Dedicated to everyone who helped to shape the present me

It always seems impossible until it's done

7 Secrets of building a million dollar empire

by

Andy Wong

ISBN: 978-981-07-8881-0

About the author- Andy Wong

Hawker assistant, direct sales, delivery assistant, waiter, sales assistant, surveyor, host, actor, radio dj, club manager and even zookeeper. These are all part of Andy Wong's experience while growing up. Andy Wong was a youth offender who was suspended from secondary school and dropped out from polytechnic before he ventured into business at the age of 19.

Till date, he has operated a pub, published a magazine, ran an events company, opened a coffee shop and started an online radio before he found his current niche in entertainment where he produces shows, seminars and events with international big-wigs ranging from Apple Co-founder Steve Wozniak to former American Idol and X-factor judge, Paula Abdul.

Inspired by Donald Trump, Andy created Midas Touch Asia Global Business forum (MTA) in 2013 with the objective of providing a platform for entrepreneurs and high net worth individuals to learn, network and be recognised. MTA features an internationally recognised leader in business or politics as the keynote speaker. (MidasTouch.asia)

His holding company, Miracle Entertainment Group Pte Ltd is valued at $10 million as of October 2013, a month after he turned 29. Today, Andy holds passion and charity as his core values, which he hopes to inspire others with.

Hear what others have to say about working with him:

Apple Co-founder, Steve Wozniak
"It's been the best trip of my life, to Singapore. All the arrangements made it smooth for me, catered to my desires... ... And, I'm going to be a real proponent, an unofficial ambassador, for Singapore business from this day on."

Former American Idol & X-factor Judge, Paula Abdul
"You were the best; you provided everything and then some. There's nothing else we could have asked for. God, you were fantastic. Thanks for taking such great care of me. I send you lots of love and look forward to working with you again!"

Grammy Award Winner of " Sometimes when we touch" Singer, Dan Hill
"I have had the greatest time of my life. Not only is Andy a superb promoter, he has taken care of anything I could conceivably need as an artist. He has also become a wonderful, caring, kind friend. And I would highly recommend any artist who wants to play in Asia, to contact Andy of Miracle Entertainment. You'll simply find no one better. My heart is crying because I have to leave here now and go back to Canada. "

Contents

Preface

I came from a very average family, except that my parents divorced when I was very young, about 3 years old. I think that's one of the reasons that made my learning journey different. I never had a role model to learn from; hence I have always been curious about the world. I remember being very excited about helping out at my grand uncle's stall at the national stadium back in 1994. I was 10 then, helping to pack syrup drinks and peddling them through the cheering crowd during the Malaysia Cup soccer matches. I never once felt tired during the job and the ultimate joy would be receiving my $10–$20 wage at the end of each match day.

To be able to earn and spend at free will, I felt empowered.

From that point on, I was determined to find opportunities to work whenever I could. I always asked my friends to come along but they were only interested in their video games. I remember my friends talking about their video games while I flipped through the newspaper at the age of 11 trying to find jobs that would hire young kids like me. I recall helping out at my uncle's BBQ chicken wing stall at age 11; selling Christmas cards at age 12; being a book delivery assistant at age 13; a Food & Beverage assistant at a cinema at age 14; doing outdoor sales at age 15; and serving as a banquet waiter and electronic sales executive at age 16.

My part time job experiences from 15 years old onwards have attributed to my present day way of life, which I will share with you later in this book.

Growing up, I frequently learned things the hard way. I got into trouble with the law at 17, got locked up for 2 weeks and sentenced to 18 months of probation and 180 hours of community service after I got suspended from secondary school. I then attended Polytechnic but eventually after failing the same module twice; never graduated. There was even a point where I was so down and out; I slept in the park for 2 weeks. Thankfully, Singapore being a garden city has great parks within the central business district (CBD) area. At my lowest point, I almost got divorced because I didn't have a single dime to support my family.

Now that you know a little about my background, you may or may not relate to my life experiences. But this is what I'm trying to say: I am just like everyone else on the street. I earned what I have today through struggle and endurance; it was by no means easy. What I'm about to share are the life lessons I've learned during my own journey.

I hope to inspire you to live the life you want. In my case, I built a million dollar company before I reached the age of 29. I work with the best in the industry and collaborate with names that I never would have dreamed possible.

By writing this book it does not mean that I am popular or debt-free. It only means that I have achieved what society defines as success.

Chapter 1: Passion

To earn your first million, sell the best that you can, and do so tireless and endlessly. Sell 1,000,000 units at $1 each or even 10,000 units at $100 each. Many people just want to sell their one product at $1,000,000. An important question to ask yourself: have you really moulded your passion into such a value?

The number one question I always ask young adults or people who want to get into business is "What is your passion?" Many stumble on this question while some give me an immediate reply. Passion is the most important element in one's life. If one has no passion, the person will be as good as a walking zombie. They will just go about their daily life not having an aim and have regrets later in their life. Those with burning passion—you can see it in their eyes, the way they talk about the topic and the desire to achieve it. Childhood ambitions are a form of passion. Do you remember yourself pretending to be a policeman, doctor or lawyer during your early years? What have become of those passions? Everyone has that passion in them, but often, due to various reasons such as family obligations, fear of failure, or even thinking that it's impossible, they stop pursuing your passion.

I remember in 2012, I had Oliver Dacourt in town for a soccer clinic at Offside futsal court. He is one such example of someone with a burning passion. He is internationally famous for playing for great clubs like Leeds United FC, Everton FC, and Inter-Millan FC. He has played alongside the greatest names in soccer, such as Zidane, Louis Figo, Patrick Viera, Nakamura, and Nakata, among others.

One incident I remembered very clearly that touched me deeply was during his first day of the soccer clinic. It had been raining the night before. I drove him to the venue, but instead of the expected 25 attendees, only two very young kids of about the age of five and six turned up. Imagine the kind of situation where an internationally-acclaimed football player shows up to a near-zero attendance soccer clinic! I was trying to find a place to bury myself to hide away from the embarrassment. Naturally, he was upset and somewhat annoyed at the situation. Despite the circumstances, he kept quiet and put on his soccer boots, stood up and said, "For these two kids, I'm going in."

He turned and walked into the futsal court and started his session with just those two attendees. For the next two hours, he displayed true professionalism and conducted soccer drills without any hint of disappointment or negativity. The session ended with their parents very impressed and obviously thrilled. Imagine yourself in the same situation—how many of you could have maintained such cool-headedness and done what Mr. Dacourt did?

As the program was shortened due to this unlucky circumstance, I immediately made plans for Mr. Dacourt to visit our Institute of Technical Education (ITE). The teacher in charge was very helpful and assembled his soccer students in less than two hours. Oliver was blown away when he visited ITE East Simei campus. He couldn't believe the kind of facilities and money invested for our students to learn, getting them ready for the working society. He then sat in a discussion with the students where the students could ask him anything they wanted. He shared his story and it was then that he revealed that passion is the most important aspect of every man's life. He told everyone that he achieved his success by pursuing his passion. He had no help or expressway to his dreams. He just kept playing his games and perfecting his skills while going through countless trials before his talent was finally noticed.

Many of us have the network and resources to earn a living while pursuing our passion, but what is it that is really stopping you from turning your passion into your career?

In my very own pursuit of passion, I starved, suffered, and was humiliated and rejected countless times before I made a living out of it.

I started my business when I was 19 years old. I had to register the business using my mother's name, as I was not of age to own a business then. I was working for an events company back in my Polytechnic days when I realized I was really interested in events and entertainment. After a couple of months, I decided to use whatever savings I had to buy my first audio visual (AV) system. I then began looking for leads, and rented them out. Business grew slowly and I took on all sorts of events to make ends meet. Clients would always ask if I had a particular item or service and I would always say, "Yes!" I either rented it from other companies or bought it so I could use it in future. Hence, our inventory grew gradually and I had to hire more employees to handle the events.

Although the company was doing okay, I often found it difficult to compete with the bigger boys. They had the brand and credentials and they could undercut you with their overwhelming inventory and low prices. I also often found it difficult to get sufficient manpower for our large-scale setups or events that required more specialized skilled workers. I was always stuck with big events with small budgets or unable to secure projects that wanted credible portfolios.

It was then I realized that I must make the company a reputable one. I studied and learned that companies that are "branded" are either companies which have taken on mega projects that made the news and set industry payers talking, or have owners who have gained fame or media recognition, so that their companies get recognized. With a choice of branding the company or branding myself, I chose the latter, thinking that it will be easier to gain media recognition since I was already hosting events and could try my luck at breaking into the TV or radio industry.

I saw a golden opportunity when Singapore's local TV station was hosting a reality comedian competition. I jumped at the opportunity and took part in it. I was lucky and managed to make it to the televised series. Of the 13 episodes, I appeared in 11 episodes, lucky me! It was during this period of time that I learned so much more about the image and stage presence one needs to have and the responsibility that comes with being in front of an audience.

After the televised series, I sold all of my AV equipment, thinking that I would change my business model and rebrand the company. Boy, was I so wrong. People only remembered us as an AV company and I had difficulty convincing them to use my emcee services. Things took a turn and our business took a nose dive for the next few months. I had to rely on very low paying shows in the hopes that they would find me good enough and use my services. Things continued to go against me and I was beginning to feel the financial pressure. At my worst, I would wake up to my car being repossessed by the finance company or the Land Transport Authority for failing to keep up with the loan or the road tax. To make things worse, there was a roadshow for which I had been hired to work for four days, but at the end of the first day, the boss told his marketing manager to tell me that my services were no longer required, and they paid me $50 for one day instead of the original sum of $400 per day.

It was at this moment that I questioned myself, wondering if I should carry on in this industry or just quit and get a decent job. I pondered for a few days and decided that from that very moment I would be the one choosing my clients and not the other way around. And in order for me to achieve such stature, I had to be among the best in my field. I went on watching every variety show on TV to see what the other emcees were doing to make them so popular and in demand. Through this period, my stomach was starving but my hunger for success and for my passion grew even stronger.

My hard work finally got recognized when I was given the opportunity to host alongside Taiwan's top variety show host Jack Wu at the grand opening ceremony of D' Kranji Farm Resort. After the show, he tapped my back and said, "I am truly surprised to see such a standard of host in Singapore!"

I have since stopped marketing myself as an event host and maintain only a regular group of old clients whom I charge a nominal fee of $300 an hour.

With great endurance and passion, you too can achieve what you enjoy doing. Your hunger for passion shall outdo your own limits.

Chapter Highlights

- To earn your first million, sell the best that you can-do so tireless and endlessly.

- If one has no passion, he will be as good as a walking zombie.

- What is it that is really stopping you from turning your passion into your career?

- Your hunger for passion shall outdo your own limits.

_____

Chapter 2: People—
Your Network is Your NETWORTH

Mr. Robert Wang, solicitor and partner of Hong Kong Tycoons Li Ka-shing, Cheng Yu-tung, Lee Shau Kee and Sir Run Shaw, told a crowd of businessmen at Midas Touch Asia 2013, an annual global business forum that I founded, "Use 'other people's money' (OPM) to turn into 'my own money' (MOM) in an honest way. Never employ unethical means, always use intelligence to make money and always place the interests of your clients before that of your own. Know your limits. Never over borrow."

If you want to be at the TOP, invest in and work with the BEST. Life is too short to hang out with people who aren't resourceful. This sentence may sound blunt but this is why business people form cliques and circles that others find very hard to penetrate.

At the same time, be very careful not to disparage people who aren't successful or who are the average Joe on the street, because you never know what may happen in the future. There is a very fine line between the working with the best and belittling average people. Get to know everyone but choose who to spend your time with wisely.

Throughout my journey, I observed that there are two things that bond business people, and if I wanted to even try to speak their language, I would have to learn about these two things. The first is drinking, the second is golf.

Both of which I have no clue about. However, I was determined to learn these essential skills because it could come in handy one day. I was pondering about how to pick up knowledge of the countless types of liquor out there and how I could increase my alcohol tolerance so I would not embarrass myself by getting drunk over a toast or two. It then occurred to me that I should open a bar and learn from scratch instead of drinking at pubs and paying others for my 'lesson'.

I then borrowed some money and rented a very simple 'ready-to-operate' pub along the stretch of the famous Circular Road, Boat Quay Area. I still remember very clearly on the day I took over the pub and the liquor supplier handed over a list of liquor that I was supposed to order to get ready for business the following day. The alcohol names looked totally alien to me. Not wanting to embarrass myself, I acted like I knew it all and ordered basically everything on the list. The supplier looked at me very surprised and asked "Otard? You mean your customers will drink this?" Not really sure what he meant, I replied simply, saying our concept was different. When the stock arrived, the Otard ended up staying untouched for the next six months on the shelf. I was literally drunk every day for the next two months, sometimes wondering what I was doing this for. When I sold my pub 11 months later, I had achieved my goal and knew a thing or two about different wines and whiskies. More importantly, I had begun expanding my social circle, comprising business owners, executives, and many very interesting people who share their stories with you when they are drunk.

I also understood the power of media right from the start. I have even classified three groups of influence in society: 1. Politicians, 2. Businessmen, and 3. Media. These three form a unique relationship amongst them. I noted how each group leveraged and depended on the other and how closely they were often associated. So it was no surprise when I jumped at the opportunity to take a 5-day radio presenter course the local Chinese radio was offering, in hopes that I could get into radio someday. I saw radio as an immediate and powerful medium that could reach out to millions.

During the course, I got to know a veteran radio presenter. He eventually opened up doors for me as a radio intern and I was then asked to join him as a part of the presentation. Knowing the power of radio, I proposed to the management a radio show featuring high net worth bosses and entrepreneurs. What could be better than being recognized for your business success and being featured as the weekly highlight of our Sunday show! Our 'Bosses Club' eventually became a resounding hit, with more than 40 very successful bosses featured by the time I left the show.

Some of those bosses eventually became my good friends, and we meet up for drinks regularly. One very established travel agency owner even told me that he is still friends with me only because I drink with him, this is because he gets to see the real personality of a person when they are drunk. Viola! My idea indeed worked for me! You never know when certain skills may be helpful so it is best to be prepared. These bosses went on to introduce me to their social circles over time. Further, with my hosting skills. I helped many overcome their fear of public speaking and hosted many joyous occasions, sometimes for free.

You see, it is very simple: I make myself useful, relevant, and add value to them when I am with them. You have to make sure that you are useful to them before you can even think of getting something out of knowing these people. Ask not what you can get, but what you can give. Following this advice, you will eventually be able to meet anyone you want.

Let me give you an example. Back when I brought in Oliver Dacourt, I knew that the Crown Prince of Johor, Malaysia was tasked with bringing back the Johor Darul Takzim Football Club to its former glory days. Our Singapore Soccer golden boy- Fandi Ahmad had been their head coach and I saw the possibility of Tunku Makohta Johor, Tunku Ismail inviting Dacourt over for a meet up session. Hence, when the opportunity arised, I brought up the idea to Fandi, who checked on the Crown Prince's interest. Before we knew it, the Crown Prince sent his car over to pick us up for an audience with him. It was a close and cozy session with the Crown Prince and Dacourt encouraging the Johor Team. We later had an informal session and got to know the Crown Prince better.

As you can see, it is VERY important to improve yourself constantly and stay relevant. Remember: whatever you do now, does affect your future.

Networks are built consistently and gradually over a long periods of time, just like your savings in a piggy bank. Make an effort to keep in touch with your network so you will not be seen as begging for a favor when you ask them for help after a prolonged period of no contact. And be sincere in all of your relationships.

I once met Grammy award winner and original singer of "Sometimes When We Touch," Dan Hill. He had a show in Singapore and his manager asked if I wanted to do a private show for him so I could get to know the man who propelled Celine Dion to fame two decades ago. I called a couple of my contacts and we eventually decided to do a charity concert with some corporate funding for the show. It was a very last minute arrangement but I eventually managed to pull it off, with more than 200 close friends and corporate partners turning up.

Such a feat would not have been possible if I had not maintained contact with these corporate friends who did whatever they could to help make the show happen. With Dan as my friend, I am only a step away from one of the greatest singers of all time—Celine Dion.

One very important point to note in getting to meet and know anyone you want is to realize that everyone has a need or a soft spot. Identify it and present them with their need. The door will naturally open for you.

I have had the chance to work with Singapore's largest pet store chain, Pet Lover's Centre. But it seemed that they lacked nothing. They have great brand reputation, an island-wide extensive network of stores, and have rejected numerous offers by large corporations to buy into their company, an indication of a very healthy cash flow. Is there anything that they even need?

On a very coincidental occasion, I found out that the Dog Whisperer, Cesar Millan, was coming to town for a show and I thought to myself- what better golden opportunity could there be? I learned that he was doing only two shows, and Cesar would be happy to meet his fans if given the chance. I then rang up Whye Hoe, CEO of Pet Lover's Centre, and asked if he would like to do a fan meet-and-greet for his customers. He was thrilled, but was put-off when told him the price of the two hour session. It was understandable coming from someone who has not engaged an international celebrity. However, the CEO understood the brand value it could add to his company. Hence, I worked out a package where I had risk involved and where I had to work hard enough to ensure I did not suffer losses. I then called Cesar's manager and explained to him the offer. And as planned, we managed to work out a deal.

The process of securing enough participants to ensure I did not lose money wasn't easy, but the event ended with everyone happy, Cesar meeting his loyal fans and Pet Lover's Centre adding happy customers. However, the original promoter for Cesar's show was not very cooperative throughout the process, making things difficult for us. But in this battle to protect our client's interest, I did what I needed to do to make sure the show turned out successful. This new client eventually became a close friend of mine and a testament of my capability.

Chapter Highlights

- Your Network is your Networth.

- Improve yourself constantly and stay relevant.

- Whatever you do now, does affect your future.

- Everyone has a need or a soft spot. Identify it and present them with their need. The door will naturally open for you.

- Law of leverage.

Chapter 3: Sell Yourself

I mentioned in an earlier chapter that first you must create value through the people whom you are mixing with. Otherwise it's nearly impossible to get into the clique. Before you can even think about getting into the clique, they have to know who you are, where you come from, and what you do- You basically have to sell yourself. But there is a very fine line between hard selling and soft selling. If you push too hard you might sometimes just break it, and by breaking it, you might just lose your one and only chance.

The client will have some form of expectation when you meet them, so first impressions are very important. How do you make a good first impression? The first impression is built from the very moment people look at you, talk to you, and shake hands with you. Even your body gestures are very important. Remember that being forced is false.

Always be very frank, if you know it, say you know it, and if you don't know it, say you don't. They will appreciate it more if you just tell them when you do not know the answer. There is no point in lying or beating around the bush. The people that you meet, that you want to mix with, like the businessmen and politicians, will know if you are lying. Do your homework before you even try to talk to these people. Do not just try to bullshit your way around. Remember to always be truthful. Along the way I've always been honest with the people around me. People have to be able to believe you for you to sell yourself.

I recently came across an article about Jack Ma, the founder of Alibaba.com. When Ma first started in IT many years ago, many people were skeptical about what he was doing. He then said, "Bill Gates once said that the computer and IT is the way the world lives . . . Is the way the world will be in the future." He had quoted the richest man in the world, and people believed in that. In this article Ma talked about him quoting Bill Gates from many years ago. He said that it was not actually Bill Gates who had said it, but that it was in fact he who had said it.

Ma explained that he was trying to leverage on the phenomenon of the most prominent figure in the world because back then nobody would believe in Jack Ma. Who would have thought that Jack Ma would be what he is today. Of course, as I say, if you envision you are what you believe, and if people believe it, it's the truth. Right now it's true, IT and computers are the way to go. Ma had this foresight and leveraged on other people.

In everything that you do, you must achieve to live up to that impression. By selling yourself you also have to live that kind of lifestyle. I'm not trying to say that you have to act rich. Rather, I would say that you constantly have to practice what you preach, because at the end of the day what you do, and who you hang out with will determine your market value.

I remember in 2011 when I first started working with Paula Abdul, Cesar Millan–"The Dog Whisperer," Grammy Award-winner Dan Hill, and other Hollywood and Asian celebrities. I would constantly update our social media sites with photos of us hanging out with the celebrities that I worked with. This created an impression of the value of our company. Even though the company was running on a negative cash flow, nobody that I talked to would believe that I was broke and had not drawn a salary for months. The shows that I booked were for clients and sponsors, people who were interested in being a part of these events. As I say, your market determines your value, and very often it's the perceived value that the public sees.

But do remember on this journey you are pretty much on your own. Do not rely and depend on anyone. On the flight to Singapore, former American Idol and X-factor judge, Paula Abdul once told me, "When you are popular and at your peak you have lots of friends but not many people will stick with you when you are down and out." Where will these so-called friends be?" She was at her peak in the 80's and 90's, and enjoyed all the fame and glamour that came along with her rising career. She soon realized the harsh reality when she suffered an injury that caused her to put her career on hold.

Most entrepreneurs start off knowing what they want for themselves. They often go into sales, either selling themselves or selling a product. Selling yourself means providing a service. How valuable you are to other people is shown by the price tag that they put on you. Let's take for example you are able to do a job of which others charge $100; taking one day to complete. If you can do it for half the price in one hour's time then that is where you have value to other people. In this modern day world of business, time is money. As such, turnaround time will be of the essence. When you have a fast turnaround time, you will have an edge over your competitors, and that's when people will look at you differently.

You must learn how to package yourself and transform yourself so you will show that you are able to add value to the people around you. People will want to know you, because you will be useful to them in future.

I built my network with my gift of the gab. When I meet new people I remember specifically what they do, and when the opportunity arises that I find someone in a similar line of business, I connect the two parties together. I DO NOT rush into doing business with them until the time is right. This connection eventually improves my relationship with them into a friendship. Over time, people eventually remember me as a well-connected young chap who is good with his words. When they find value in me, I will naturally find a place on their contact list!

Everyone knows that Asia is a very big market. When I entered the Asian market, people like Huang Pinyuan and Alex To were already very established and there was no need for them to know me. So when I met them for the very first time, they asked me what I did. I told them I was in entertainment. They asked what sort of entertainment I was in, and I told them I booked Hollywood celebrities for events and concerts. Everyone knows that the world capital for entertainment is Hollywood. Hollywood is the place where all the artistes want to go to get signed. Look at PSY, although he created his phenomenon in Asia, the first place he went to get world recognition was Hollywood, and that is where he made his mark.

When an artiste gets to know me, I tell them very straightforward what I do. I told Huang Pinyuan and Alex To, "If there is a chance you want to work with any

Hollywood artist or if there is any chance that you want to do some projects with them, it is something which I think I can be of value and I can help you." These people immediately registered me as someone with Hollywood contacts. You have to keep in mind that these celebrities, businessmen and politicians whom you meet, have many opportunities to get to know people at various social functions. They meet tons of people. People who are richer than you, more handsome than you, prettier than you and in many ways more capable than you.

You first must believe in yourself before you can even portray the image that people can trust you, and that people can walk with you. Remember that mental poverty is worse than financial poverty. Even if you had $1 million but you don't believe in yourself, you will soon end up with nothing.

Most people do not know the value of money and how difficult it Is to make money. There are many cases of second generation multimillionaires squandering their money. They do not know what they are doing and many times feel empty from within. That is why mental strength is very important. Studies have shown that if you are mentally strong, you can overcome anything. Having a strong mind-set is an additional value to selling yourself, because you are going to keep failing and keep trying until you find a place in this modern society.

It is the people that you mix with, the way people look at you, and the price tag that people put on you that matters. If you portray that you are a professional in the things you do and show your value, then you are on the right track to create the value that people see in you. All this takes time. Remember to build your success in the same amount of time it takes to destroy it. As the saying goes, easy come easy go. So take your time to evaluate your current situation before making your next move.

In 2008, I went to Hollywood for the very first time. I remember very clearly the first man I met, whose name I shall not mention here. When I passed him my business card he just couldn't been bothered and put my card down onto the table. When I greeted him, he didn't even bother to say "hey", or ask, "Where are you from?" He wasn't the least bit interested in me, as he was big in his own ways.

I told this guy, "I want to bring Hollywood celebrities to Singapore for a concert. Who do you have?" Immediately he picked up my card and said, "Hello!" Then he said, "Basically I have anybody you want." The guy later sent his assistant to see me in my hotel. I was given a brochure of the different celebrities they work with, ranging from Madonna to J-Lo.

Everybody has a need. If you are able to feed their need, people will commit to you. That guy knew that Hollywood celebrities are very expensive, not something the average company could afford as it would easily cost $100,000 for the average celebrity to come to Asia. Thus, not many companies would have that kind of budget to pay for their own company event. In this case I understood how the whole ball game worked.

Now you have to find your own strength in creating your own persona, your own value. It helps to join groups. When you meet new people, tell them your ideas because you never know what might come out of it. Good ideas are remain only ideas unless they are put into action- something which I'll talk about later in the book. There is always a chance that somebody will buy the idea. If somebody buys the idea then you are on your way to your next step in success.

Remember to continue to focus on what you want to do. Continue to share your passions with the people around you. Remember the book *The Secret* states that *The law of attraction* creates life-changing results such as increased wealth, health, and happiness, when we think and feel positively. The corresponding frequency is sent out into the universe that attracts back to us events and circumstances on that same frequency.

Chapter Highlights

- Envision: you are what you believe.

- Expectations are a form of first class truth. If people believe it, it's the truth.

- Your market determines your value.

- Rely and depend on no one.

- Forced is false, be frank.

- Mind over body.

- Mental poverty is worse than financial poverty.

- Net worth is perceived value.

- Build your success in the same amount of time you take to destroy it.

Chapter 4: Opportunities

Procrastination was a big issue when I was writing this book. It took me so long to come up with the idea to eventually take my thoughts and transform them into words. I advise people to travel whenever and wherever they can. Every meeting, every trip, every conversation is an opportunity. Just to give you an example, when I first went to Los Angeles in 2008, I didn't know what was in store for me, but I did know, for sure, that I would meet people on the trip. These people could potentially be very helpful to me in my career.

As luck would have it, I met the guy who had lots of Hollywood contacts that I described earlier. Many years down the road, my friend was at an integrated casino resort in Singapore, and I met him there. When I arrived, he was actually talking to the resort's producer of entertainment. Little did I know that they were preparing for the grand opening of a theme park.

I told him I had some friends in Hollywood that might be able to help him. He said that he had been looking for some celebrities to attend the event. So, as luck would have it, they later commissioned me to bring in Hollywood celebrities for the grand opening of Universal Studios. It was thanks to my meeting in Hollywood years earlier that I was able to make this connection.

Another time, I was supposed to accompany my family to my daughter's dance competition. I was hesitant to go, but when I did, I met my daughter's friend's father, Mr. Terence Ng. We talked and surprisingly, we had chemistry. We didn't really keep in contact much until one day he called me and said he wanted to meet for coffee. There, we discussed our business interests. He eventually became my investor at a point when I was at my lowest. That was also when we first created Midas Touch Asia.

Terence was very instrumental in the project. He pumped in money when no one believed in it. The project lost money, but he was still a big supporter of the event. He became the pioneer batch of investors. He also brought in two other friends who invested money in the event. This event has added value to our holding company with a professional evaluation of S$ 10 million and attracted interviews from major international medias. This event has since opened up many doors to me. These are examples of the many opportunities that can come from meeting new people.

As I mentioned, you must sell yourself. Tell people what you are doing so when an opportunity arises, there is a good chance you can work together. Having said that, whenever there is an opportunity to travel, go back and revisit your contacts, be it local or overseas. I joined the ruling political party Youth Wing many years ago, and we travelled to Malaysia. I made a few new friends from the Malaysia ruling party. We exchanged cards, but nothing happened until much later.

I happened to be in Kuala Lumpur in 2013. As a matter of courtesy, I called up my friend from Malaysia and told him I was in town and asked if he wanted to meet and catch up. He agreed and we arranged for that. Little did I expect that he would call me again that night to say, "Hey, Andy,

I've got an important friend I want to introduce to you. Are you free tonight, at 11 PM?" I said, "Wow, that's very late." Nonetheless, I went ahead. It turned out I was meeting the Malaysian Prime Minister's son, Mr. Nazifuddin, that night. We had a good hour conversation that lasted three hours. We discussed our business interests and we managed to click. I then invited him to Singapore to speak at our upcoming Midas Touch Asia 2013. He was hesitant, but after the meeting, I followed up with an email. He eventually accepted the invitation and came to Singapore. After the event, we continued to talk and we realized that there were things we could work together on. He is now my business partner in Midas Touch Asia.

As I say, the opportunity arises when you least expect it. Do remember, opportunities are only meant for people who are ready. With the right direction, with the right angle, the right parties will eventually meet. This is what it's all about. You have to be ready. When the opportunity arises, you grab it. As they say, "Opportunities don't come knocking twice." So, look around to see what opportunities are available. Never say no, always keep an open mind. Keep going out there to meet people. Keep talking to people because eventually, as I said, that is how you find out who needs something. At the end of the day, you will not regret what you have done, but you will regret what you have not done.

Get out there and start meeting lots of people. Li Ka-Shing once said that, when you are poor, you have to go out there and meet people. When you have nothing to lose, it doesn't hurt to continue meeting new people. When you're rich, then you can stay home more often. But you have to build a strong foundation for your business first. I have learnt that opportunities can always arise when you least expect them. There was a time when I was having a casual conversation with my friend when he said that he was going to Malaysia the next day to look at a factory. I asked if I could go along so that I could take a look at it too. We went together to look at this factory, it was a dying business. . After a while, we realized that we should work on this business together.

We then got the rights to the brand, Welmix, which is a 30 year-old brand in Malaysia. It has become the pioneer, and in fact the owner of the factory became the first person to have created instant cereal. We decided to go into the coffee business. We started a company in Singapore called Welmix International Pte Ltd., which deals with the sales and marketing of instant coffee. Coffee is a business where the margin is very thin. It's a commodity item where people will want it on a daily basis once they are used to its taste and flavour.

One very fine day when I was in Malaysia, I received a call. "Hi. I'm Prince calling from Tata Coffee," he said. "My managing director is coming down to Singapore and would like to meet up with you to explore if there's any possibility that we can work together." In my mind, I was thinking "Yeah, okay," because we'd get calls like that from time to time. But the managing director eventually came and I met up with him. I was introduced to their company, Tata Group. Tata Group is the largest private company in India that deals with almost everything and anything you can imagine. They're the second largest company with billions of dollars of assets. So, I made a new friend, the managing director from Tata Coffee, and now, we're looking forward to seeing how we can work together in the near future.

To wrap up, just like Justin Bieber says, "Never say never." Before he made his big break, he posted his video onto YouTube, where he was discovered. Now he pursues his passion and brings his music to the world.

Chapter Highlights

- There are a lot problems in the world today, you just need to solve one and you will be rich.

- Travel whenever and wherever you can. Every meeting, every trip and every conversation is an opportunity.

- With the right direction and angle, the right parties will eventually meet.

- The man below mixes around to find out what people want and need. The man on top looks around to see what is available.

- You will not regret what u have done but what you have not done.

Chapter 5: Think Big and Focus

I'd like to dedicate this chapter to Donald Trump. I would say he pretty much influenced the way I act, the way I think, and the way I do things today. I read a book that he wrote, *Think Big and Kick Ass*. In this book he talks about how thinking big is a very important element of who he is today. In it, he says something that made a lot of sense. He says if you're going to think, you might as well think big. It's true. We are thinking every day. We are thinking about lots of things. We are thinking about how to create a business, how to make our lives better. We're thinking about so many things. They say to shoot for the stars. When you think big you naturally have bigger goals. You have bigger ambitions. When you think big you are able to play the big game with the big boys. That's what it's all about. When you start out doing small business, eventually you want to do big business, so you might as well think big.

I will give you a very good example. Midas Touch Asia was originally created to do a conference seminar keynote speech featuring Donald Trump. The Midas Touch idea actually came from the name of the book that he and Robert Kiyosaki co-wrote together. In *Midas Touch* they talked about the touch of gold, and the different elements that are required to turn your business into a multimillion dollar business. On a recent trip to China, I saw HSBC's advertising line, "Even the smallest business can go global." This really makes sense to me as business has evolved in a very big way. With the internet you can do business from your home. People can use your product or services without you ever having to even leave your house.

When you're planning for a business, you need to think about what happens if it goes big one day. You need to protect your business. You need to make it unique. If you want to launch a big ship, you have to go where the water is deep. This is common knowledge. You can't launch a big boat in a stream. You can't launch it in the river. So you basically have to go into the big market. A lot of people can get comfortable just being small, so comfortable, so it's a matter of choice. You decide whether you want to be the big fish in the small pond or the small fish in the big sea. But high risk equals high gain and the bigger the sea, the bigger the chances of making it big.

The word "history" is made up of "his-story", right? To make history, to leave a legacy, you must create your own story. You have to aim to be the champion because nobody in this world will remember who is second. We all know Lance Armstrong, the seven time world champion cyclist. Yes, he cheated; he took drugs to make him a champion. But have you ever remembered who came in second in all of those races? Nobody ever remembers. Look at Formula One with all those big name champion drivers like Hamilton, Alonso, and Schumacher. All it takes is that one time. Become a champion and it will propel you to the next level. Remember you can fail a thousand times, but all it takes is one success. People will remember you for life.

A lot of people say they can't do this or they can't do that. Remember, your achievements are only limited by your creativity. Today Apple is a phenomenon. Everyone somehow or another has used an Apple product before. Apple has changed the world and revolutionized how people live. Every evolution and revolution happens because of people with the ability to think big and take action. This year when I was creating Midas Touch Asia, I wanted to bring in Donald Trump, but because of budget constraints and many other factors, I couldn't get him. I told myself that the speaker for Midas Touch Asia should be a multi-billion dollar company founder or a billionaire. Billionaires are a very unique group of people. They are the trendsetters and the game changers. They can make things happen. As of March 2013, there are 1246 billionaires on the Forbes list. What makes these thousand people so unique? They have the ability to think big. They have the ability to think outside the box. They're always thinking many steps ahead of all the other people out there. These would be the people to attract a crowd to our event. Businessmen like to be inspired and learn from these giants. Hence, when the big boys are at an event, it brings in quality partners and builds a strong name.

For those who are still thinking: Are you up to it? Are you old enough? You will never be prepared. Come on. This is a fact of life. We procrastinate and we wait and wait for things to happen. When you think big, you must always be ready to take action. Remember this: If you're good enough, you are old enough." But "If you're old enough, it does not mean you are good enough.

I beg your pardon? You might say. I repeat: If you are good enough, you are old enough. Look at Mark Zuckerberg. He created Facebook from nowhere when he was in college.

Today he is the world's youngest billionaire. Can you say that he's wrong? No. But in business there's no right or wrong.

When I tried to revamp my company's image, I realized the only way to be big was to do something different. You have to stand out from amongst your peers. During that year when I started to make that change, there were six thousand other organizations calling themselves event companies. I thought, anybody can be an event company. You just take out a phone book and coordinate a few things: then you are known as an event manager.

What makes me different? I learned a lot after I brought in Paul Abdul for the Theme Park grand opening. I realized that after that show, people looked at me differently. People thought my company was a big company because people saw Hollywood as being the big time with big names. So I told myself, *OK. Let's do this.*" Moving forward, I tried to connect companies with the big names. I tried to do events, concerts, and seminars with high profile personalities. You need to know that there's this law of leverage. You need to leverage the high value people. The high powered person can bring you up to the next level. This is part of moving up the ladder of success. Sure, you may not have the money, but the ability to think big will allow you to find the right people to be part of your projects. When people know that you're out to do big things, big, realistic things, people will then associate you and your name with the big reputation. Don't be afraid to bring that new idea out onto the international platform. I have personally learnt that if you see what others don't see, then it has a value. If you are able to see what others are seeing, I'm telling you, other people can do a much better job than you. So set a goal that you can't achieve. Because that is the only way you keep yourself moving forward. There is a saying, "the only constant is change." Ideas are everywhere. You must constantly be on your feet and thinking about what the world is looking at next. The willingness to think is something no one else can give you. When you shape your success mind-set, you actually imagine your success.

However, while you are thinking big you must remember to also be realistic. You have to take baby steps to achieve the big picture. I'm not asking you to create success overnight because it's not realistic.

With that, I hope I'm able to influence you to think big. I've always wanted to bring in the big names like Donald Trump, Madonna, Oprah Winfrey, and Celine Dion. I work very hard to find a way to get closer to these people. Take for example, when I brought in Dan Hill. I know he was the one who gave Celine Dion her big break. It is good to be connected to him, should I think of creating a tour for Celine Dion. If I do not have the volume, people will not talk to me. I was always the second tier of consideration as a concert promoter. I wanted to be the first guy these people came to talk to when they were planning their concert tour. This is why I say the only way to break through is with volume. When I had the volume then people would look at me seriously. I told myself I was going to run Celine Dion's Asia tour. So I began to talk to people. I called Dan Hill's partner. He said it could be done; it was all about the dollars and cents. I just needed to pay them the right amount of money and then we could talk about the Asia tour, because she would not come out for just one or two shows. That would be too small for her. I said, "okay, let's do the Asia tour." When I did the calculations, this Asia tour was worth more than 10 million U.S. dollars. I had to be able to put my money where my mouth was. This was a rare opportunity. I then came across a private equity firm and told him about the project. He was excited, and offered a $10 million investment.

I was trying to bring in Donald Trump for Midas Touch Asia 2013 but as the event was very new and I was unable to find the right investors, I decided to bring in Apple co-founder Steve Wozniak instead. Apple is a legend and there's a story to be told. I had to bring in someone who was of international interest. When I brought in Steve Wozniak, he attracted international media attention. BBC. Thomson Reuters. Swiss National TV. All of them were asking for an interview slot, which provided lots of coverage. When deciding on a partner, the choice to partner with Asia's premier news network, Channel NewsAsia, was critical. People know that it is very difficult to work with Channel NewsAsia because they do not co-host an event. They either host it themselves or you pay them to be the supporting TV station. They do not work with private sectors just like that. They were impressed because I showed that I had the big names. Having Channel NewsAsia as our co-organizer lent credibility to our company.

All this boils down to the initial ideology of thinking big. I envisioned these people coming on board, and these people eventually came on board to form my big picture.

Many times all you need to do is just to get the right people in place. Everything else will eventually fall into place. Stay focused on your goal.

Remember, business is like a car travelling on a road. You meet others in all shapes, colors, and sizes. Some faster, some slower. It's just the same with other companies. You see big companies, MNCs, listed companies. Do not envy the big and flashy ones. Reaching your destination is what matters most because along the way some will breakdown or get into accidents. Very few recover and continue their journey. Do what you need to do to get there, as no two cars, no two businesses, will get there at the same time with the same route. When you focus, you might be able to find a shorter route with just an average car. When crisis hits, big companies are usually affected the most. It's just like along a busy road, in times of accidents and traffic jams, you realize it's the motorcycles that are able to cut through and reach their final destination first. You just have to do what you need to do.

Chapter Highlights

- If you want to launch a big ship, you must go to where the water is deep.

- If you are good enough, you are old enough. Always aim to be the Champion , because no one remembers number two

- If you see what others don't see, then it has a value... If u see what others also see as valuable then someone else can do better than you.

- Your limitation is only down to your creativity.

- Set a goal which you can't achieve.

- History is always written by man. His story.

- When shaping your success mindset, imagine your success, not pretend and imitate it.

- Business is akin to a car travelling on a road, you meet others in all shapes, colors and sizes, some faster, some slower. Do not envy the big and flashy ones. Reaching the destination is what matters most. Some break down or meet with accidents along the way. Few recover and continue the journey. Do what you need to do to get there as no two cars will get there the same time with the same route. Focus and you may find a shorter route with an average car.

- The willingness to think is something no one else can give you.

_____

Chapter 6: Readiness and Planning

In 2008, I had a chance to meet our former President, His Excellency Mr. S.R. Nathan, and former Health Minister Mr. Khaw Boon Wan. We had a chat. I realized that these people speak with profound knowledge, and I actually couldn't even keep up with what they were talking about. After the event, I told myself, I must empower myself to gain as much knowledge as possible. Knowledge is power. Content is king. What people can't take away from you is the daily learning, the knowledge that is kept within you. That thirst to learn has to be with you regardless of what you do; be it studying business or learning about an organization that you are in. Remember I spoke earlier about opportunity, because when you're ready and you've planned well, that is when the opportunity knocks. Then you set up a plan to do what you need to do. Nobody plans to fail. People only fail to plan. Of course, imagination creates knowledge. Whatever you can imagine is what will interest you. These are things that inspire you to learn more so that you can understand the bigger picture.

ABC. Always be curious. You have to listen to what others have to say. You have to keep learning along the way. Business is like an F1 race. You need to endure and take over at a crucial point. To take over at the most crucial point, you need to be able to have the extra surge. The extra turbo. In this case the knowledge that comes along with you will be your turbo. Many years of planning and skill will enable you to take off at that very crucial point.

It's just like when I did Midas Touch Asia, I had everything in place. I had the network. I had the protocol. I had the system. What I lacked were the tickets sales. I was supposed to sell tickets for the event, and I was promised by the China group and an Indian group that X amount of delegates would come in for the event. I did my due diligence. I calculated. I presumed that it wouldn't go wrong, and it wouldn't have if everything had gone according to plan. However, what can go wrong will eventually go wrong, it is something that you can't control. In this case, I had to change. I got back on a plan to change the whole concept. It was supposed to be a full-fledged conference whereby business entrepreneurs and corporate leaders came to listen to Midas Touch Asia. Unfortunately, because it was a new event, nobody believed in the event, so I could only manage very little registration and we would have lost a lot of money. So I included an awards segment, where local companies were evaluated and I partnered with the right partners. . The companies were given awards for their enterprises. This worked well because eventually you manage to attract all the good friends, and reputable companies come on board, some of which are multimillion and billion dollar companies. When these companies came on board they brought along their guests, who gave us the praise for having such a successful event.

Great mentors are like expressways to success. I have met many people along the way who have taught me very well. They taught me things I would never learn in school.

One such instance was with Paula Abdul. I had in-house photographers following the entourage to make sure that I had videos and photos documenting the trip. That was the very first time I had brought in an international artist. I thought by taking photos it would be very helpful for my future portfolio. It was then that Paula Abdul called me over. She told me, "Andy, you need to understand that we like to preserve our privacy because you never know where these pictures might end up going to. I know that they are in-house photographers, but yet there could be incidents where these photos might leak out to the public." Her assistant came over and said, "Paula, I think you shouldn't be so harsh on Andy." Paula responded, "No, I meant well. I want this guy to learn the industry. I want him to be able to succeed with other celebrities and artistes in future." I learned that lesson very well, which is why I say great mentors are like short cuts. They are expressways to success that teach you things that you do not normally learn in life.

To the banks, I was just so small that very often, they wouldn't even be interested in talking to me. Back in those days when I was being paid by the client to bring in Paula Abdul for an event, I couldn't get the money to the bank in time, so I called a good friend of mine, Dato' Dr. Johnny Ong. He was actually the first big-time businessman I had met. He told me that with a TT wire slip I could go to the bank to get them to release the money because that piece of paper equals money. So true enough, I went ahead. I got the money ready in cash and brought it over to Hollywood.

During Steve Wozniak's interview with the media, he highlighted that in the early days of Apple, Steve Jobs would get very excited and would share with those around him his plans for the company. When he got fired and rehired later on, he learnt the lesson of secrecy; to keep every development under wraps until the product is ready to be released to the world. He would fire anyone who leaked information of their new products to the public.

From this, there is another lesson we can glean: do not launch your final product until you are absolutely sure that it is ready for the market. It takes daily effort to plan and be ready. You have to consider the worst-case scenario and you have to be ready for it. There are many things we do not know. Many of the bosses and entrepreneurs that I know of personally, despite running multi-million dollar companies and businesses, always believe in respecting the professionals and using the best person for the job. This is because the best person for the job is a form of insurance to ensure that nothing goes wrong.

You get a certified public accountant to do your taxes. You get human resource professional to hire the best people. These are the things that will ensure that your company structure is being taken care of. Likewise, on a smaller scale, even if you are renovating your house, you hire the best people to do the floors, the best people to do the walls, and the best people to do the cabinets. This is the same theory. Don't hesitate to pay well for people who are able to do the best job for you. They are there to make sure that the job is done to the highest standard. That standard equates to your public image and your reputation. Your reputation is at stake.

When Steve Wozniak came to Singapore, he came three days in advance. Although his engagement was just for one hour, he wanted to be fully prepared. From this you can see the way he does things. He was being a true professional. He took a day to recover from the jet lag, and another day for media interviews. On the very next day he wouldn't even consider doing anything in the morning. He said that he does not like to do anything on the day of his speeches, until after the event. He said no two speeches of his are the same because he will prepare on the actual day of the event. He will feel the environment and try to make sure that what he says makes sense and applies to the current situation. He wakes up and he takes a good deal of time to prepare his speech. And you could see from the audience that his speech was truly mesmerizing and insightful. People waited the whole day just to hear what a great man like him would say.

Chapter Highlights

- ❖ What's the worst case scenario? If you can take it, do it!

- ❖ You will never be ready.

- ❖ Respect the professionals.

- ❖ Hiring the best person for the job is a form of insurance.

- ❖ Knowledge is power, content is King. Empower yourself.

- ❖ Business is like a F1 race, endure and overtake at the most crucial point.

- ❖ Sales is the only way to fortune, find something to sell.

- ❖ Imagination creates knowledge.

- ❖ ABC Always be curious-- listen to what others got to say and keep learning.

- ❖ You can't control what you can't control.

- ❖ Great mentors are like expressways to success.

Chapter 7: Execution Without Fear

By now you know what you want to do. Do something that you are passionate about and set out to achieve it at all costs.

I'm sure you know of people who have felt betrayed by their friends, or that their friends have done them wrong. It is really important to focus on your goals. At the same time, decisions that you make along the way might make some people unhappy, but sometimes you just have to do what you have to do. Very often great decisions are unpopular and are only appreciated until much later.

I'll give you an example. In March, 2011 when I told the producer of the integrated casino resort that I had Hollywood contacts, he told me to look for an artist that would be suitable for his event. He gave me a budget of $250,000 Singapore dollars. That was a huge sum to me back then, and I knew if I could do this job successfully I would be able to change the future course of my company.

With the client's list of prospective interests, I narrowed my choices down to Michelle Yeoh, an international movie star. I spoke to her manager for almost two hours at the lounge of Four Seasons Hotel. We almost made a deal. Later that month, I gave the client a list of artistes that would say yes to attending the event.

I thought everything was going very well and according to plan. But closer to the event, the producer called me and said they were not going to give me the job because my company was very new and had no track record or relevant experience. It was one of those instances where your high hopes are dashed and your world comes crashing down around you. I had to cancel Michelle Yeoh, and her manager was quite upset and even wrote to the integrated casino resort's producer to verify that this engagement was indeed cancelled by them and not me. This incident almost ruined our reputation as the new kid on the block. I was thankful when Michelle's manager eventually accepted my explanation.

A couple of weeks down the road, exactly 10 days before the theme park's grand opening, the producer called me back and said, "Andy, we need you to confirm Paula Abdul now." I said, "What?! You said you wanted to cancel!" I told him "Look, this is not going to work. We have only 10 days left and there's nothing we can do now." The producer responded, "Andy, we have to do this, tell me your terms, I'll try to accommodate and fulfil them." So, I hung up and gave it serious thought. They would have tried talking to every other company out there and I was the only one able to get the contract since the big players were obviously not willing to risk it.

At that moment, it was a do or die situation. If I made it, I was on to the next phase of my journey, but all the odds were stacked against me. The stakes were much higher. I then realized that since we I was already at my lowest, it couldn't get much worse than this. Since it didn't really matter anymore, I decided to take the job.

I decided to take the dive and called the producer. I said, "Okay, I will take the job but instead of $250,000 they're going to ask for half a million Singapore dollars because it is last minute and I'm not even sure whether Paula Abdul still wants to come to Singapore." Of course, they were not very happy, saying that I was jacking up the price in the 11th hour. I told them that we either do it or move on. It didn't matter to me at that point if I was going to get the job. It was really going to be a test of my capabilities. But finally the producer called and said, "Okay, come down tomorrow, the contract is ready."

Immediately after signing the contract, I called my U.S. counterparts that Paula Abdul would be paid to come to Singapore. I had also put in an offer for American Idol winner Fantasia Barrino to come to the event as well. But because it was just too last minute, they had to cancel on us and I had to look for another American Idol to replace the original performance.

The funds were transferred to me the very next day. But that was a weekend and banks do not work on weekends. I told Paula Abdul's manager that I would transfer the money to them on Monday. The manager said that things did not work like that in the United States, and that I needed to pay in full before the artist would even board the plane.

Here I was trying my best to work things out, to make sure the artist turned up, and he was going through a set of terms and conditions stipulated in the contract. Then the U.S. bank said that anything over $50,000 had to take five days to clear. By then it would be too late. When I called the producer to tell him that I had to reject the job due to the near- impossible timeline I was facing, I was given a very straight reply. He told me I signed a contract and that it was my responsibility to carry it out. In that moment, I realized everything was at a standstill. I would be sued if I failed to honour my contract.

When I turned up at the bank on the following Monday, I requested to speak to the Branch manager and I asked him to release the money. The only thing I could do was to withdraw the cash and bring the entire sum of money to the United States and hand it over to Paula Abdul's manager so she could board the next flight to Singapore.

The branch manager was in shock and said, "You're asking for a few hundred thousand dollars in cash! How are we going to give it to you in just a short time?" But he called the bank's headquarters and finally managed to release the money to me at about one o'clock. I had to get to the airport for my check in before the gate closed at 2pm. While I went to the airport, I was lucky to have a friend waiting at the bank, who then brought me the bag of cash once it was ready.

Imagine this; I actually brought along S$300,000 in cash! Wow. That was the largest amount of money I had seen in my life. I didn't even have time to change it to U.S. dollars before I brought it over. I landed at LAX airport 8:30 PM. The next flight out was the following day at 11pm. I had exactly 26 hours to make things work!

The very next day I literally drove around all of Los Angeles looking for a place to exchange money, and finally managed to change enough money to pass on to Paula Abdul and the rest of the performing team. Through this transaction, I lost $17,000 Singapore dollars. But yet I thought to myself, *Phew*!

To make the long story short, when I came back to Singapore, Paula was happy that I had sorted everything out. She later nicknamed me the "Mafia" because only the Mafia in the United States carried around so much cash! I made sure that my Singapore team was ready to receive her from the airport. I provided first class service; from the moment she landed in Singapore, I wanted her to feel like a queen. I even hired security personnel that were former bodyguards to Prime Ministers, so that everything was fit for a royal.

However, the resort's in-house security tried to stop me from providing security for her, as they told me they were capable of handling everything. I was not confident in them. Unbeknownst to them, I decided to deploy our own security officers. My instinct paid off when Paula was mobbed by a group of reporters on the red carpet. The in-house security looked totally helpless! I made the decision for our own security to step in and they managed to get her out of the mob in less than a minute. In situations like this, you must be able to carry out decisions that are critical to the success of your job.

Those few days were incredible. Working with a world class artist really opened my eyes to how entertainment is done at an international level. I learned a lot from that trip. Meanwhile, there was this part-time employee hired by the integrated resort to take care of and chaperone Paula Abdul. She didn't know the job and she created a lot of problems for us. On opening night, Paula Abdul was to do a dance number for the audience. She was supposed to guide her backstage. Instead, the employee grabbed Paula by the arm, which caused her a lot of pain, and Paula was very upset. I had to pacify Paula while at the same time making sure this employee of the resort didn't come close to us. At the end of the day I got the lady sorted out, she was detached from the entourage and everything went on smoothly.

Remember what I said about adding value? There was one occasion where I was at the commercially important passengers (CIP) complex of the airport and Paula was trying out a massage chair, which she loved. Without her knowledge, I called my friend Dr. Derek Goh, who actually sent an email to Mr. Ron Sim, Founder of OSIM, and maker of the massage chair. I then brought Paula to an OSIM outlet and got her to choose something for herself and for her fellow X-Factor judges as a memento. She was, of course, very pleasantly surprised. She felt that I had the capability to grow in this industry. When she left, she left me her mobile number and her contact information, and we are still in touch today.

The story didn't end after the event. The integrated casino resort felt that I didn't fulfill my duties to what was stipulated in the contract and they wanted to sue for US$175,000. I thought that was incredible because I didn't even make that much money! I then called for a meeting. This was a case where I had to remember that these were big people but I knew that elephants couldn't kill ants. Elephants are huge but have you ever seen an elephant kill ants in a stampede?

I told the resort's counsel that they did a background search on me, and the reason why they didn't let me to do the job initially was because my company was too small. I told them they could sue me for US$175,000, but if they did, it would be through bankruptcy. I also told them that if they sued me it would make them look very, very bad.

Finally, after many rounds of negotiations, they came back and we ended the whole issue amicably with them demanding US$30,000 as compensation. I only offered S$5,000 as the final settlement amount. While they accepted the payment of S$5,000, they insisted that our company still owed them US$25,000, which they will get back as discounts when we do a show for them in the future. So, with that, the whole saga came to a close. However, it was an episode that really tested me on the way I managed a crisis. Every difficulty teaches you something, some life lesson that you'd never be able to learn if everyday life was just simple.

People think that the road to success is a straight line. But let me tell you- that it's just life, a maze made up of left turns, right turns, and 180 degree turns. It is always constantly changing. There is no straight road to success. When I brought in Cesar Millan, the Dog Whisperer, and Chugg Entertainment was his main promoter. They made things very difficult because I didn't go through them officially to get the deal. I went through Cesar's U.S. manager and Chugg wanted me to buy insurance because they claimed that by having Cesar Millan out of their supervision there was a possibly that Cesar might get injured and in the event of such injury, Cesar would not be able to perform his two sold-out shows. I did everything I could to make things work. I told the CEO very clearly that I did not have to comply with them, and if they were unhappy they could go talk to Cesar's manager, because I bought the show directly from him. You do have to know that at certain times you need to stand your ground and be very firm with what you need to do.

What will go wrong will eventually go wrong because many times, regardless of what business you are in, it will happen when you least expect it. Very often the mistakes are created by people you know very well and that you assume would deliver to your satisfaction, so don't assume. You have to personally make sure that things are being done to your satisfaction because your reputation is at stake. There are some multi-millionaires that I know personally that wanted to retire early, so they prepare for succession. However, the minute they step down, the company revenue dropped by 50 percent. Remember, your name and reputation, are everything.

Chapter Highlights

- Break the rules, make mistakes. Failures are meant to mould you into a bigger success.

- Elephant can't kill ants.

- You can fail 1000 times but all you need is 1 success and you are there. You only need to excel in 1 thing in your life.

- Every difficulty is an opportunity in disguise.

- Set and achieve at all cost.

- Failure is not an option.

- Great decisions are usually unpopular and appreciated until much later.

- Extraordinary= Extra Ordinary.

- Don't fight a war in their territory

- Expect the unexpected. Fear the known not the unknown. What will go wrong will eventually go wrong

Conclusion

Entrepreneurship is an ongoing process. You need to steer your own boat to do the things that will make a difference in your life. You need to be extraordinary in other people's lives. When choosing a mainstream career, you have to continually revolutionize the way you think. You have to innovate, to think outside of the box. That is how Apple managed to become what it is today. If there is no precedent, if it hasn't been done before, then break the rules. Make mistakes because it's through the University of Hard Knocks that we are able to learn so that we do not commit the same mistakes again.

These words are meant to move you toward bigger success. I have met many businessmen along the way, and some of them have become good friends but some also hated me, said I was arrogant or proud, and honestly at times at times I even find myself pretty irritating as well! But all you need to do is keep on moving, prove them wrong, and eventually they will see that what you're doing is correct.

People will only look at you when you're successful; nobody cares about the journey to success. You have to fend for yourself, be very passionate about your goal, stay focused, and achieve it at all costs.

When I was a television host I told myself that I wanted to be successful because I wanted to help people around me. Only if I am successful will the people benefit. When I spoke, people listened, so I had the influence over many things. With that influence I could do good things. A Singapore politician once said in the Parliament, "Politics is about power, but when you have power don't abuse it, use it to do good things to help people."

For those looking for a mentor, feel free to write to me and I'd be very happy to share with you my experiences, and if you've got great business ideas, I'll work with you to see that your ideas materialize. Keep envisioning the route of your success. If you're passionate about a certain career, whether it is sports, or being a lawyer or a doctor, there are steps you need to take to get there. Don't procrastinate. Stop thinking. Put your ideas into action.

"It always seems impossible until it's done." -Nelson Mandela, 1918-2013.

Connect with me on fb.com/mr.ndwong or follow me on twitter @mr_ndwong .

Days as a TV artiste

Hosting the community National Day celebrations in 2009

On Air "Live:" as a Radio DJ

Interviewing for the Bosses' Club program

With Former President of Republic of Singapore His Excellency Mr SR Nathan

With Former American Idol and X-factor Judge Ms Paula Abul

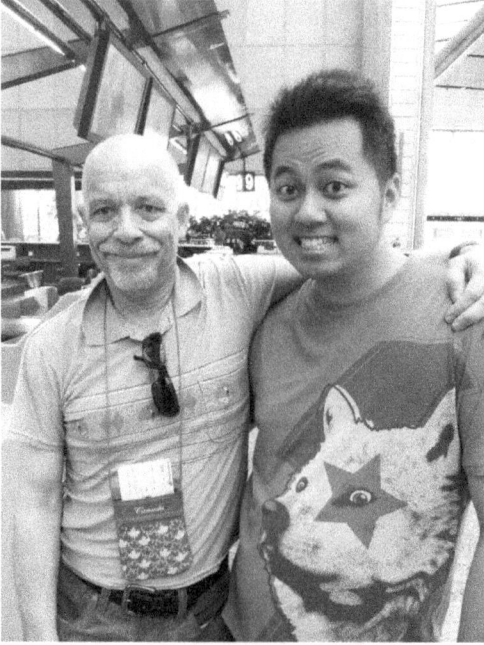

With Grammy Award-winner, Singer Composer of Greatest Hit of All Times "Sometimes when we touch" - Mr Dan Hill

L: French soccer star former Everton, Leeds United, AS Roma & Internazionale player- Olivier Dacourt

R: FIFA 100 Netherlands soccer star, former Ajax, Milan, Juventus, Barcelona, Internazionale and Tottenham Hotspur player- Edgar Davids

Olivier Dacourt with Singapore's soccer legend- Fandi Ahmad

Olivier Dacourt sharing his experiences with soccer club members at ITE Simei

With Tunku Mahkota of Johor, Malaysia (Crown Prince)

-Tunku Ismail

Olivier Dacourt sharing with the Johor Darul Takzim Team

Cesar Milan autograph session

Overwhelming turnout for Cesar Milan Meet & Greet

Delivering an opening address to 300 high networth individuals and enterprenuers at the 2013 inaugural Midas Touch Asia Global Business Forum

Forum Session with Mr Robert Wang, solicitor and partner of Hong Kong tycoon Li Ka-shing, Cheng Yu-tung, Lee Shau Kee and Sir Run Shaw

With Mr Nazifuddin Bin Dato' Seri Najib Razak and Ms Puteri Norlisa Bte Dato Seri' Najib Razak

Answering questions from the floor about business in Malaysia

Apple Co-founder Steve Wozniak delivering his keynote speech

Question and Answer Session with Steve Wozniak

Steve Wozniak in discussion with Singapore's Minister of Environment and Water Resources Dr Vivian Balakrishnan

www.ingramcontent.com/pod-product-compliance
Lightning Source LLC
LaVergne TN
LVHW051801080426
835511LV00018B/3374